Reed Hastings and
Netflix

INTERNET BIOGRAPHIES™

Reed Hastings and
Netflix

CORINNE GRINAPOL

ROSEN
PUBLISHING®

New York

Published in 2014 by The Rosen Publishing Group, Inc.
29 East 21st Street, New York, NY 10010

Library of Congress Cataloging-in-Publication Data

Grinapol, Corinne.
Reed Hastings and Netflix/Corinne Grinapol.—First Edition.
    pages cm.—(Internet biographies)
Includes bibliographical references and index.
ISBN 978-1-4488-9525-0 (library binding)
1. Netflix (Firm)—History. 2. Hastings, Reed, 1960– 3. Streaming
technology (Telecommunications) I. Title.
HD9697.V544G75 2013
384'.84—dc23

                                                        2012040829

Manufactured in the United States of America

CPSIA Compliance Information: Batch #S13YA: For further information, contact Rosen Publishing, New York, New
York, at 1-800-237-9932.

Contents

INTRODUCTION

When Reed Hastings created Netflix as a DVD-by-mail Internet business in 1997, a time when just a sliver of the American population owned DVD players, he was already thinking ahead, planning for an idea that wouldn't really be feasible for almost a decade: video streaming. It is this instinct for being able to imagine what the future of media consumption could look like, and a commitment constantly to evolve, that has made Netflix a household name in the home entertainment business.

Reed Hastings turned Netflix into the largest DVD-by-mail company in the country and then proceeded to lead its streaming service in the same direction by staying in front of technology trends. His influence extended beyond his own organization—his ideas have changed many aspects of the entertainment and technology business, from how we pay for movies to how we choose what to watch. Many of Hastings's ideas, like monthly subscription fees for unlimited movie viewing, are so prevalent today because he was the one who introduced them and made his competitors follow suit.

For a long time, it seemed that Hastings's talent for taking Netflix in the right direction—as demonstrated by ever-rising membership numbers, high stock prices, and

With a simple business idea based on mailing DVDs in slim packages to customers, Reed Hastings, founder and CEO of Netflix, changed the way people rent movies.

year after year of operating in the black—was fail-proof. As it often happens, just as Netflix had reached the height of its success, the fall came, quickly and steeply. Hastings's leadership was challenged in 2011, when a new, unpopular policy led to a significant loss of members, sliding stock prices, and a host of critics claiming Netflix was dead.

Learning from his mistakes, Hastings continues to steer the still-recovering company in new directions, focusing now on creating original programming and developing Netflix's international presence. During this challenging time for the company, when it faces a new round of competition from companies eager to get into the video streaming market, can Hastings keep Netflix on top?

CHAPTER 1

The Early Years

Reed Hastings was born Wilmot Reed Hastings, Jr., in Boston, Massachusetts, on October 8, 1960. Hastings's father was a lawyer in the Department of Health, Education, and Welfare during President Richard Nixon's administration. If this department sounds unfamiliar, it is because it underwent a split in 1979 to become two separate departments: the Department of Health and Human Services and the Department of Education. In an interview with Amy Zipkin from the *New York Times*, Reed Hastings recalls a perk of his father's position: Hastings's family was invited to Camp David when he was about twelve years old. Camp David, located in Frederick, Maryland, is the president's country home. Since Winston Churchill's visit to the camp in 1943, the site has been one of historical significance, with many foreign leaders having made visits there since. While Richard Nixon wasn't there at that time, Hastings remembers an interesting detail of this trip: Nixon's "gold-colored toilet seat."

The Charles River in Massachusetts separates two cities central to Hastings's childhood: Boston, where Reed Hastings was born, and Cambridge, where Reed Hastings went to school.

Hastings attended Buckingham Browne & Nichols School, or BB&N, a private day school in Cambridge, Massachusetts. Other notable alumni from the school include actress and producer Mindy Kaling and journalist Peter Beinart. Hastings graduated from BB&N in 1978 and took a one-year detour before entering college, working as a door-to-door vacuum salesman.

When deciding what college to choose, Hastings said in the interview with Amy Zipkin that he was looking for a "small liberal arts school." He ended up going to Bowdoin College in Maine, choosing to study math because he "found the abstractions beautiful and engaging." At Bowdoin, Hastings was head of the Outing Club, a club that still exists, whose members participate in outdoor activities such as canoeing and rock climbing.

FROM THE MARINES TO THE PEACE CORPS

While at Bowdoin, Hastings joined the Marine Corps Platoon Leaders Class. As the son of a civil servant, Hastings believed it was a good way to give back. The Marine Corps Platoon Leaders Class is a program available to college students who are interested in entering the Marine Corps as officers—second lieutenants, specifically—after graduation. Students spend their summers training at the

A candidate undergoing training at the Officer Candidate School in Quantico, Virginia, is addressed by the platoon sergeant. Training takes place over the summer for either six or ten weeks.

Officer Candidate School in Quantico, Virginia, a program that combines leadership training, military-related study, and a physical training component that includes obstacle courses and long, arduous hikes.

While attending the course in the summer between his sophomore and junior year of college, however, Hastings realized the Marines weren't for him. His style of thinking wasn't a match to the type of deference to authority required by the corps. Even then Hastings exhibited the kind of thinking that seeks to examine a way of doing something in order to figure out if that is the best way. In the Marine Corps program, it was Hastings looking at the method of making beds and packing backpacks. Hastings's questions weren't met with much enthusiasm, and he decided to go into a new direction and leave the Marine Corps program.

Hastings found a new way to contribute. After applying and being accepted into the Peace Corps, he left the United States in 1983, on the day of his graduation from Bowdoin, to start his service in the Peace Corps. The Peace Corps is a program started by President John F. Kennedy that encourages Americans to volunteer throughout the world, working with other countries in areas such as education, agriculture, and health care. In addition to helping communities worldwide, another goal of the Peace Corps is to promote understanding between the United States and other countries. Hastings spent two years and seven months in Swaziland, a small country in southeast Africa bordering Mozambique and South Africa, teaching math to high school students. Hastings recalls the area in Swaziland where he taught as one without electricity, where most people still wore traditional clothing in bright colors.

It was during Hastings's time in the Peace Corps that he made the decision to go to graduate school. He was still in Swaziland as he began to prepare his application, starting with a two-hour bus ride to the capital of Swaziland, Mbabane, where he was able to take his Graduate Record Exam, or GRE.

Hastings would later credit his time in the Peace Corps with giving him the courage to try and accomplish seemingly daunting tasks. As he said in an interview in *Fortune* magazine, "Once you have hitchhiked across Africa with ten bucks in your pocket, starting a business doesn't seem too intimidating."

LIFE IN THE VALLEY: GRAD SCHOOL AND BEYOND

Hastings arrived in California in the summer of 1986 to get his master's degree in computer science at Stanford University in Silicon Valley. The school had not been his first choice. Hastings had wanted to stay on the East Coast and go to MIT, but he hadn't gotten in. At first, the palm trees of southern California felt very different from the

East Coast educational backdrops he was used to. It took him a week to get used to it. In a *USA Today* interview with Jim Hopkins, Hastings reportedly told his parents back in New England, "You'll never see me again. I've found nirvana." The computer science program at Stanford would turn out to be useful for the direction of Hastings's career because of the way it complemented its computer science education with business training.

After graduating from Stanford in 1988, Hastings went to work for Schlumberger Palo Alto Research, a technology research lab. A few months after Hastings began working there, Schlumberger, Inc., which owned the lab, announced that it was going to close the lab in Palo Alto.

Hastings's next move was in January 1989 to a technology start-up company called Coherent Thought, where he worked as a software engineer. After about a year at the company, Hastings moved on to start his first company.

THE FIRST START-UP

In 1991, at the age of thirty, Hastings started his first company,

The campus of Stanford University is set in California's Silicon Valley. Like Reed Hastings, many Stanford graduates go on to create well-known businesses in the area.

called Pure Software. Originally, Pure Software created tools for programmers using UNIX. UNIX is a computer operating system—it makes it possible for a computer, with all its programs and operations, to function. The initial products that Pure Software developed were focused on helping programmers and developers de-bug their software, meaning it helped developers locate the kinks and issues that were preventing the software from running efficiently. The company gained success early on, creating a need for Hastings to expand the company. The way Hastings did this was by purchasing already existent companies and combining, or merging, with them. The mergers also resulted in a few name changes for the company. When Pure Software merged with Atria, the company changed its name to Pure Atria.

By 1996, the company now known as Pure Atria was doing very well, making over $2 million in profit by the spring of 1996. However, while the company's business was doing well, its employees weren't faring as well. Hastings said that the excitement of working at the company when it was still Pure Software had waned through the years until the company consisted of employees who considered Pure Software just another place to work.

A lot of the problems were due to the mergers, which happened so quickly that a lot of new employees were suddenly thrown together. A lot of the leaders at the top of the

Lessons Learned

"I had the great fortune of doing a mediocre job at my first company," Hastings told reporter Michelle Conlin in an interview for *Bloomberg Business-week*. Why would Hastings call his mediocre performance a fortunate occurrence? Because it gave him a large set of examples and scenarios to draw from when figuring out how to prevent the same kind of company culture from creeping into the next company he started, Netflix. Hastings looked at his experience at Pure Software as a chance to figure out what he had done wrong and make sure the same thing wouldn't happen at Netflix.

For the few months that Hastings stayed on after Rational Software purchased Pure Atria, he was able to observe and learn how Rational Software ran a company. One thing Hastings noticed was that many of the people leading Rational Software had been at the company for a very long time, as opposed to Pure Atria, where, because of the turbulent, sometimes combative atmosphere, people wouldn't stay long. A lot of this had to do with how the company treated its workers. In his interview with Michael V. Copeland, Hastings described his observations of Rational Software: "It was so different how they operated—the level of trust and the quality of interaction between them was impressive."

This made Hastings realize that was the type of environment he wanted to create for his new company, and to achieve this goal, he'd have to be proactive about doing so. Hastings also made the decision to change how he interacted with employees, including when it came to really hearing out new ideas without passing immediate judgment.

organization would come into and leave the company very quickly. Hastings described the atmosphere in the *Fortune* interview with Michael V. Copeland as, simply, "chaos."

Realizing the organizational environment wasn't ideal, and believing his own leadership had to do with it, Hastings told Jim Hopkins at *USA Today*, "I tried to fire myself—twice."

The solution to the problem ended up coming from outside the organization. In 1997, a rival company called Rational Software ended up buying Pure Atria. The purchase was made with stocks instead of money, so although Hastings was supposed to make $890 million from the sale, the stocks dropped when the purchase was announced, and Hastings ended up making about $525 million. Still, this was enough money to put toward founding Netflix, which is what Hastings would end up doing with the funds. After the sale, he stayed at the newly merged company for a few months before leaving, giving him an opportunity to witness an entirely different company culture than the one that had been the norm at Pure Atria.

CHAPTER 2

Planning for a Future That Hasn't Yet Arrived

The story of how Reed Hastings came up with the idea for Netflix is a tale that he has told and retold in many interviews. It starts in 1997 with a video Hastings had rented—*Apollo 13*—that, after being six weeks overdue, had

The 1995 movie *Apollo 13* starred Tom Hanks, Kevin Bacon, and Bill Paxton. Hastings has stated in interviews that he believes it was this movie for which he owed a late fee.

accrued a $40 late fee. He had forgotten about the video and was worried about telling his wife. That same day, as Hastings was heading to the gym, he thought about how a gym operated, with a flat fee customers paid that allowed them to come and go as they pleased, and thought how much better of a system that was.

It was those two small, everyday life experiences that formed the seed of an idea for Hastings's new company. To turn that idea into a functioning business, Hastings used his former CEO experience and educational background in computer science. He started to think about how he was going to make his idea, a video-by-mail company, happen. Then, a friend told Hastings about DVDs. In 1997, DVDs were brand-new; it was the first year DVDs and DVD players were being sold in the United States. Hastings decided to test them out. After buying a number of CDs from Tower Records, a media entertainment store, Hastings placed the CDs, removed from their cases, in envelopes and mailed them to himself. A day later, the CDs arrived undamaged.

Hastings asked Marc Randolph to join him as a cofounder and started gathering the members of his team. On August 29, 1997, Netflix was officially incorporated, meaning that it officially established itself as a business under the law, but it wasn't known as Netflix yet. The first official name for the company was Marc Randolph's idea, based on advice he had received from one of his mentors when he and Hastings were struggling to come up with a name. The mentor told him to first pick a name so horrible that it could never become the default name chosen, and then work on figuring out a name everyone could get behind. And so, at the beginning of its life, Netflix was known as Kibble, Inc., as in dog food.

When Hastings started Netflix, it was not just an opportunity for him to run a new startup, it was also a chance for him to take the lessons he had learned from running Pure Atria Software and become a different kind of leader than he had been there. Hastings wanted to make Netflix a place where smart people were motivated to work effectively, were continually seeking ways to improve and innovate, and would stay for a long time. In 2009, Hastings posted for public view a slideshow entitled "Netflix Culture: Freedom and Responsibility." This 126-page slideshow put into words the lessons that Hastings had learned from his time at Pure Software and the new vision he had for life at Netflix.

A NICHE MARKET

With 87.9 percent of households in the United States owning a DVD player by 2010 according to Nielsen, it is hard to imagine that when Hastings decided in 1997 to make Netflix a DVD-only company, just 7 percent of households in the United States had DVD players, according to *Fortune*. DVD players had just been introduced to the U.S. market that year; not even Hastings had heard of them before his friend told him about them. The videocassette recorder (VCR) dominated the home video market, just as Blockbuster Video dominated the video rental market. Not only were DVDs something of a rarity, Netflix was also going to be an Internet-only company at a time when just 18 percent of households in the United States had Internet access, according to the U.S. Census Bureau. As it stood in 1997, Netflix's customer base was going to be a small, specialized group of people. Netflix was created for a niche market.

The reason why Hastings chose to build Netflix around DVD rentals was simple: VHS cassettes were too expensive and too bulky to pack and ship by mail. By contrast, the cost of a DVD shipped inside of a small square envelope was just thirty-two cents.

The success of Netflix would depend on technologies and trends—Internet, DVDs, e-commerce—that would need to keep growing in order for Netflix's customer base to expand. However, even during the very earliest days, Hastings had his eye on a technology that wasn't yet viable. He believed that eventually, most people weren't going to watch their movies through DVD or VHS players, but were going to access them through the Internet. This is why, as Hastings told Patrick J. Sauer in *Inc. Magazine* in 2005, "We want to be ready when video-on-demand happens. That's why the company is called Netflix, not DVD-by-Mail."

Reed Hastings poses with two spools of DVDs. From the early years, Hastings sought to create a large selection of titles for the Netflix library to stand out from the competition.

THE EARLY MODELS

Despite the fact that the idea for Netflix was inspired by—and was a reaction to—a late fee, Netflix's first service wasn't really different from a standard store rental model. When Netflix's Web site went up in May 1998, customers paid $4 for each video, plus $2 for shipping. It wasn't long, however, before Netflix implemented the plan that looked more like that business idea Hastings had come up with on his way to the gym. In September 1999, Netflix introduced its subscription plan, in which customers paid a flat monthly fee for an unlimited number of movies. Under the new plan, customers signed up to become members of the Web site, created a queue of movies in which they marked the movies they wanted to watch, ranking them in order of preference. When customers watched and returned a movie, the next movie in their queue would be shipped to them automatically in the square red envelopes. If a customer's top choice wasn't available, the next available option was sent. It was the subscription model that really began to bring in the customers.

As Netflix was developing customer-oriented innovations, it was employing similar innovations on the business side as well. Traditionally, video rental stores would purchase videos directly from a studio or a wholesaler at a fairly high cost, and then keep 100 percent of the profits from the rental fees it charged customers. Because purchasing videos in large amounts was expensive, video stores generally kept a small stock of each movie. The selection would be small as well, skewed to the blockbusters and

Workers process DVD orders at a Netflix distribution center. Centers like this make it possible for DVDs to get to customers as rapidly as possible.

other well-known movies that stores assumed would be most likely to be rented.

Since Netflix's focus was on the small but expanding DVD market, and it was one of the first companies focused exclusively on DVD rentals, Hastings wanted Netflix's selection of DVDs to be comprehensive and updated continually as new DVDs came out. Since customer satisfaction was key for retaining customers on a subscription-based model, it was also important for Netflix to purchase a good number of DVDs of each movie title in order to keep wait times down for customers. Purchases on this scale would be expensive under the traditional model, so Hastings sought a different way.

A new member of Netflix's board of directors, Bob Pisano, a former movie studio executive, helped Hastings arrange meetings with a number of movie studio executives. These meetings resulted in Hastings creating revenue-sharing agreements with a number of movie studios, a practice that the video rental store company Blockbuster had pioneered. Under these arrangements, which began in 2000, Netflix would purchase DVDs from a studio at a lower cost. In exchange, when a customer rented a title from that studio, Netflix would pay the studio a certain percentage of money that it made from its customer subscription fees. Not all of Netflix's purchases fell under revenue-sharing deals, and new acquisitions were a mix of revenue sharing and direct purchases.

RESEARCH AND EDUCATION

During its early years, Netflix worked quickly to carve out its identity, establishing a distinct employee culture, implementing its subscription model, and finding ways to lower the cost of DVD purchases. In 2000, Netflix created what was to become another important piece of its identity: its movie recommendation system, Cinematch. Focused as Netflix was on providing an expansive range of offerings, Cinematch was a good way to introduce its members to titles that they may never had heard of.

In 2012, Neil Hunt (right) and then vice president of project engineering John Ciancutti discuss the future of Netflix. Ciancutti moved to a job at Facebook later that year.

How Cinematch Works

The Cinematch recommendation system uses an algorithm to suggest movies to subscribers. An algorithm is a series of steps, or set of instructions, used to complete a task or solve a problem.

Cinematch uses a subscriber's reviewing history and combines it with the reviews of all its customers to determine how likely a subscriber is to like movies he or she hasn't yet seen.

Imagine, for example, you, as a user, have just given the highest rating possible, five stars, to a movie. To make a recommendation for you, Cinematch processes your rating using a lot of different angles. It looks at other movies you rated highly. It breaks down the components of the movie you just saw into different characteristics. It looks at movies with similar characteristics and the ratings other viewers have given those movies. With Cinematch, all this information and more is run through a specific series of steps, or inputs, to get the output, which is Cinematch's recommendations for you.

The more reviews users make, the better the system becomes. As of 2002, Netflix made eighteen million recommendations per day. The spread of titles Netflix offered was highly effective: as of 2002, of the 11,500 titles it had available, 11,000 of those had been chosen by members.

It was also a good way for Netflix to keep its costs down under the revenue-sharing deals. The percentage of its subscription fees that Netflix would have to pay a studio under the revenue-sharing deals was determined by the frequency with which customers watched titles that were part of the deals; the more customers that rented those titles, the greater the cut of its subscription fees that Netflix would have to pay to the studio.

What Netflix wanted to avoid was a situation where most customers were renting the same small selection of well-known movies. With Cinematch, Netflix could encourage customers to try a larger variety of titles, especially lesser-known titles.

For Reed Hastings, 2000 was also the year of an important personal achievement. Governor Gray Davis of California appointed Hastings to California's State Board of Education and made him president of the board the following year. The State Board of Education is responsible for governing the California Department of Education. One of its main roles is to set policy, such as deciding what students in California's public schools should be learning on a broad level and what tests to use to measure progress.

Hastings's interest in education dated back to his experience teaching math as a Peace Corps volunteer but more recently had been put to use with his involvement in the Proposition 39 campaign in California. Proposition 39, which passed in 2000, centered around how districts voted to purchase school bonds, used to repair school buildings.

Hastings was president of the board for three years. Many of his actions as president were admired. Some of his decisions, however, would ultimately not sit well with some of California's state senators. At the time, a portion of students in California who didn't speak English were being taught in their native language. Hastings believed that even those students should be taught in English for two and a half hours a day. When it came time to reconfirm Hastings, the senators opposed to his stance on bilingual education joined to deny him a return to the board.

CHAPTER 3

NFLX

On May 23, 2002, a new stock symbol appeared on Nasdaq's flashing electronic stock ticker: NFLX. The previous day, Netflix had made its initial public offering, or IPO, turning what was previously a private company into a public one. What does it mean to be a public, or publicly traded, company? For one, it means that people are able to buy and sell shares of the company on the stock market. By purchasing a share, a person lays claim to a stake in the company; he or she now owns a portion of the company and is referred to as a shareholder. The more shares a person buys, the more ownership he or she has in the company. When a company is private, a relatively small group of people have ownership of it, and it is usually the founders who decide who gets an ownership stake.

A company that decides to go public finds itself with new responsibilities. The company now falls under the regulation of the U.S. Securities and Exchange Commission

Nasdaq headquarters in New York City. That Netflix chose Nasdaq as the exchange through which to trade its stock makes sense, since Nasdaq is a popular home for tech stocks.

(SEC), the government department in charge of regulating the investment industry. A public company is required to send annual and quarterly reports about the state of the company and its finances to the SEC and shareholders. These reports are available for anyone to read. If someone wanted to know, for example, how much money Netflix made last year, that information is available on the SEC Web site, which posts the company reports Netflix creates.

With all these requirements, it may seem strange that a company would want to go public, but there is one huge advantage: the proceeds from the sale of stock during the IPO goes to the company. This becomes especially important when, as was the case with Netflix at the time of its IPO, a company is in debt and hasn't yet turned a profit.

In 2002, when Netflix tried to go public, it was not the first time. Its first attempt at an IPO, in April 2000, had failed to get enough investors interested. This partially had to do with timing. In the 1990s, a new class of companies that existed solely or primarily on the Web, known as dot-coms, emerged. As these companies went public, they were met with a lot of enthusiasm by investors, and during the years known as the dot-com bubble, their stock prices soared. Many of these companies offered their services for free and weren't making any money when they went public, operating on money from private investors known as venture capitalists. The idea behind these companies was

People in Times Square watch tech stocks fall during the dot-com bubble. Increased interest rates were one reason the bubble happened when it did because this made it harder for companies to borrow money.

that they were going to focus on growing their membership quickly and figure out how to make a profit later.

Bubbles eventually pop, and the dot-com bubble burst spectacularly. After the Nasdaq stock exchange—which most dot-com companies were part of—hit a high on Friday, March 10, 2000, stock prices started falling. When some of those companies, after years of not making a profit, went bust, and it became clear that many of the remaining ones would not make it, stock prices for dot-com companies plummeted, as did confidence in Internet companies. When Netflix first tried to go public in 2000, it was too soon after the bubble. Internet stocks were still falling, and investors were wary.

PayPal, which went public the same year as Netflix, is an Internet company that allows individuals and businesses to pay for goods and services and process purchases over the Internet.

THE DEBUT

When Netflix made its second attempt at an initial public offering, only one other major Internet company had gone public since the dot-com bubble: PayPal. As Reed Hastings would later explain in an interview with Steve Gelsi of MarketWatch.com, he felt that the company was in a better position in 2002 than it had been in 2000: "We've now got a very predictable, stable and growing business model. Two and a half years ago it was a lot more erratic. We felt

How an IPO Works

When a company makes the decision to go public, it usually comes after taking a long reflective look at itself, its finances, and the direction that it wants to take. If the company thinks it's ready to withstand the scrutiny that comes with being a public company, there are a number of steps it must take before it makes its home among those other businesses experiencing the highs and lows of the stock market.

The first step is to gather the team that will work on the IPO. This usually includes the CEO, CFO, and other key members of the company. The team begins to work on Form S-1. This is the form that all companies that want to go public must file with the SEC. The S-1 gives the SEC and potential investors information about the company and its finances, and it ensures that the company's practices fit in line with the requirements for a public company. It also lets the SEC know the tentative price and amount of stocks it plans to sell.

As Form S-1 is being prepared, the company will hire underwriters. The underwriters help complete the form, advise the company on how the stock market is doing, and suggest the price and amount of stock the company should sell. The underwriters are also responsible for getting investors interested in buying the stock.

Once Form S-1 is complete, the company's board of directors must approve it, after which it is submitted to the SEC. At this time, the company also decides what stock exchange it would like to be a part of and sends a request to that exchange.

The SEC will review the form and send it back with questions and comments the company then needs to respond to. Once approved, the company goes on an IPO road show, making presentations across the United States to generate interest in purchasing stock.

Finally, the company registers the stock, and the SEC puts the IPO into effect. The first groups to buy the stocks from the IPO are the investment banks and professional investors the company has made agreements with during the road show. It is those investors who will trade the stocks on the stock market. The company makes money from the sale of the stocks during the IPO but doesn't make money once the stock trades on the market.

mature enough as a business to have the public scrutiny and be successful."

On March 6, 2002, Netflix filed Form S-1 with the SEC, its first step in going public. This form let the SEC know the company planned to go public and provided much of the information investors needed to decide whether to buy shares of the company. The financial management firm Merrill Lynch & Co. was the main underwriter, responsible for getting investors interested in purchasing shares.

Netflix made another important change in March 2002: the company previously known as Netflix.com dropped the .com in its name and became, simply, Netflix. With its new name, Netflix distanced itself from the failed dot-com companies of the bubble years.

As Netflix readied itself for its IPO, there were, as Reed Hastings had said, aspects of the company that had improved since its first attempt: both Netflix's subscriber base and its sales had risen. However, although Netflix's sales had improved, the company had yet to make a profit. It was losing less money than in previous years, but the company was still in debt. In fact, Netflix was planning to use a portion of the money from the IPO sale to pay down its creditors.

Netflix stated in its IPO filing that it didn't expect to make a profit "for the foreseeable future." The ability of Netflix to make a future profit would depend in large part on the continued growth of subscribers. As of the filing, Netflix had 11,500 movie titles, over 600,000 subscribers, and almost $91 million worth of debt.

Given a range of $13 to $15 within which to set its offering price, Netflix decided to go with the top amount.

On May 22, 2002, Netflix filed its IPO, selling 5,500,000 shares for $15 each, making $82.5 million on the sale. The initial sale a success, the future fate of Net-flix's share price would now be left to the stock market.

The next day, when the Nasdaq stock exchange opened for business, NFLX, Netflix's symbol on the exchange, was ready for trading. At the close of the trading day, the shares of the stock had risen to $16.75 from $15, a good start for a young stock in a cautious market.

IN THE BLACK

Despite a promising first few months, culminating on July 5 with a stock high of $18.19, the young life of the NFLX stock started to run into trouble. In August, whispering began about Blockbuster testing a new online rental service. In October, Wal-Mart also started to test its own online subscription service. The possibility of competition in Netflix's specific corner of the market—online subscriptions—caused stock prices to drop. By January 1, 2003, Netflix stock was selling for $6.60. It may have seemed like a bleak time for Netflix, but the fate of NFLX on the stock market told only part of the story.

Netflix continued to run at a loss for all of 2002. This meant Netflix's revenue, or the total amount of money that it made—mostly from its monthly subscription service—was less than what it cost to operate the business.

Before Wal-Mart decided to officially enter the DVD rental market, a mere whisper of a rumor that it was going to do so was enough to negatively impact Netflix stock.

These costs included paying employee salaries, storing and shipping DVDs, and marketing and advertising, among other expenses. The good news was that the numbers kept getting better. Netflix was making more money and losing less of it. By the end of 2002, its revenue for the year was $152,806,000. The previous year, Netflix had made $75,912,000. This was a 103 percent increase in revenue. Meanwhile, Netflix's net loss for 2002—or the amount by which its total costs and expenses were more than its revenue—was $21,947,000, down from $38,618,000 in 2001.

The main reason that Netflix's revenue for 2002 was up by so much was due to its growing base of subscribers. By the end of 2002, Netflix had 857,000 paying subscribers, compared to 456,000 in 2001. Like its revenue, this was a 103 percent increase, which made sense, since all but 1.3 percent of Netflix's revenue came from subscriptions.

Netflix credits its large title selection and responsive customer service for keeping its subscribers happy and having them stay with the service month after month. As for the growth of subscribers, that was an example of a bet on the ever-forward march of technology working out. When Netflix started its subscription service in 1999, just four million households in the United States had DVD players, representing 7 percent of households in the United States. By the end of 2002, the number had risen to an estimated forty million households with a DVD player. For Netflix, the increase in the number of homes with DVD players meant the number of people who could potentially become Netflix customers was growing quickly.

In 2003, a year after Netflix had debuted its IPO, the company posted its first ever profit. With a $6,512,000 profit for the year, Netflix was in the black.

CHAPTER 4

Competition

In a 2005 *New York Times* interview with Gary Rivlin, Reed Hastings said that he regretted going public so early. The regret came not because the IPO was unsuccessful but precisely because it was successful: "In hindsight, what triggered Amazon and Blockbuster to compete with us is they could see how profitable we were and how fast we were growing," Hastings told Rivlin. But before either Blockbuster or Amazon would attempt to compete in Netflix's backyard, Wal-Mart made the first move. On October 15, 2002, Wal-Mart announced that it had started to test its own DVD-by-mail service. Like Netflix, Wal-Mart was going to offer a subscription-based plan that charged customers a flat monthly fee to receive DVDs by mail without due dates or late fees. In what would later turn out to be an important difference, Wal-Mart was pricing its plan at $18.86, $1.09 cheaper than Netflix's plan, which was then $19.95 for unlimited DVDs that customers could receive three at a time.

In June 2003, Wal-Mart's DVD-by-mail service graduated from its small test phase and became available to everyone. This marked the entrance of Netflix's first direct major competitor. There were already other Internet-based DVD-by-mail services in existence, but they were small, and Netflix was the market leader. Wal-Mart was the first with the resources available to pose a serious threat to Netflix. If Hastings was concerned, it was because Wal-Mart had the capability to wait it out as it attempted to catch up to Netflix.

According to an article in the *New York Times*, Hastings told reporter Nicholas Thompson, "No one is going to out-hare Netflix. Our danger is in a tortoise attack." By 2003, Netflix had been operating Cinematch and its subscription service for quite some time. In June 2003, Netflix was well on its way to the growth figures its 2003 Annual Report to Shareholders would describe: 18,000 DVD titles in its library, 1,487,000 subscribers, revenue-sharing agreements with over 50 studios or distributors, and its movie titles had received over 3 million customer ratings. Netflix had a huge head start over Wal-Mart, or any other new competitor. The effects of Wal-Mart's entry into the market could take time to materialize.

BLOCKBUSTER GETS IN THE GAME

In a 2001 interview with Tom Mainelli in *PCWorld*, Hastings was asked to describe the typical Netflix subscriber.

Netflix Patents Its Business Model

During the same month that Wal-Mart debuted its subscription service, Netflix had news of its own. On June 24, 2003, it announced that it had received a patent for its subscription model. A patent is a type of protection given by the government for a person's, group's, or organization's intellectual property. Intellectual property is property that is intangible, that is, it can't be touched. This includes ideas, designs, inventions, and ways of doing things.

The patent process can be a lengthy one, but for those who have created a unique invention, design, or idea, the effort is worth it to protect their work. It begins with the applicant (or a patent lawyer) completing the patent application form required by the United States Patent and Trademark Office (USPTO). Once the form is filed, and the filing fees are paid, the USPTO reviews the application and does extensive research based on the information on the form. The USPTO must make sure that the application is in full compliance with patent law and that the idea or invention does not already exist anywhere in the world. The invention must meet three important criteria to be granted a patent. According to the USPTO, the invention must be "new, useful, and nonobvious."

Once a patent is granted, it lasts twenty years. During that time, anyone who copies, uses, or sells the invention without receiving permission from the owner of the patent could be fined. Receiving permission to use someone else's patent may involve the payment of royalties, or a fee for use, to the patent holder.

Netflix's patent covered the process it used for receiving DVDs from customers and sending DVDs to customers. If Netflix wanted to, it could use the patent against its competitors to make sure they didn't copy Netflix's highly efficient system.

Hastings responded, "The average Netflix customer is someone who loves movies and hates Blockbuster. That's not everybody, but it is a large section of America and it crosses all kinds of demographics." In 2001, Netflix was a small organization working in what was still a niche market. In 2002, after Netflix's IPO, Blockbuster started paying attention. In August 2002, Blockbuster—which at that point had a traditional rental model in which customers paid a specific price for each rental and had to return it within a set amount of time or else incur a late fee— had begun to test out in a few cities a subscription service similar to Netflix's. The service, called Blockbuster Freedom Pass, allowed customers to pay a monthly fee to rent an unlimited amount of videos without late fees. However, this program was for in-store rentals only.

Although Blockbuster was not yet offering a DVD-by-mail service, news of its Freedom Pass service caused Netflix's stock price to drop. Reed Hastings, however, saw this as an opportunity for Netflix to prove itself. In a *New York Times* article by Bob Tedeschi, Hastings said, "Until a company has faced competition and won, its mettle is uncertain with investors. We're properly not given that credit yet because we haven't been tested." The test was about to begin.

Blockbuster's arrival on the online video rental market came on August 11, 2004, when the company introduced Blockbuster Online, its new DVD-by-mail subscription service. Like Netflix, the service allowed customers to create an online queue of titles and receive and return DVDs by mail for a flat monthly fee with no late charges. The cost for unlimited rentals that arrived three at a time was $19.99. To make itself more competitive, Blockbuster leveraged its physical rental stores by also offering new subscribers a monthly coupon for two free in-store rentals, although customers also had to be in-store members to get this deal.

In interviews, Hastings indicated that competing against Blockbuster was going to be a big challenge but

Workers process DVDs at a Blockbuster distribution center. Netflix's patent on DVD processing has a potential influence on how competitors such as Blockbuster design their centers.

ultimately healthy for Netflix. In a *New York Times* article, Geraldine Fabrikant reported that Hastings believed there was enough market demand for both Blockbuster and Netflix to survive.

PRICE WARS

In June, just weeks before Blockbuster announced its new mail subscription service, Netflix had raised the price on its three DVD unlimited plan to $21.99 from $19.95. In explaining the price increase, Hastings said in a press release the revenue from the price increase was going to be used to make improvements to its service.

The $21.99 plan was short-lived. After Blockbuster announced that its three DVD plan was going to be cheaper than Netflix's, costing $19.99, it was just a short time before Netflix dropped its own price. This triggered a price war between Blockbuster, Netflix, and Wal-Mart, as each company tried to entice customers to its own plan.

On October 14, 2004, in a company press release, Netflix announced its plans to lower the price of its three-DVD subscription plan to $17.99 starting November 1, 2004. This was partially in response to the lower prices offered by Wal-Mart and Blockbuster, and partially based on rumors that Amazon.com was going to enter the DVD-by-mail market. Just four days later, on October 18, 2004, Blockbuster announced that it was dropping the price of its three-DVD plan to $17.49. In a press release, Blockbuster's CEO John Antioco made clear Blockbuster's intentions with regard to competing for customers with Netflix: "In the first six weeks since the service launched, we've signed up more subscribers than Netflix signed up in its first year and a half of existence. Additionally, we are

Blockbuster attempted to lure customers away from Netflix with low-priced DVD-by-mail plans. In addition, Blockbuster offered another perk: customers could rent DVDs in the store each month using coupons Blockbuster sent them.

confident that we will end this year with more subscribers than Netflix had after its first three and a half years." The war over prices was a race for customers.

On November 5, 2004, Wal-Mart made the next move, dropping the price of its three-DVD plan to $17.36, making it the lowest priced three-DVD plan. This didn't last long. Blockbuster, determined to have the lowest prices, dropped the cost of its three-DVD plan to $14.99 in December.

Although the price wars were clearly good news for customers who watched their plans get cheaper, it wasn't nearly as beneficial for Netflix. For one, the popularity of Netflix's plan, combined with the lower subscription price, reduced its profit significantly. Due to improvements Netflix had made to its service, the majority of customers were getting their DVDs within a day, which meant they were able to view more DVDs per month than they had previously, driving up Netflix's shipping costs. In addition, with more customers viewing more movies, revenue-sharing costs went up. Even with these increased costs, Netflix had its second consecutive year in which it made a profit, and its membership was up to 2.6 million subscribers. In spite of this, investors were still wary about the ultimate effects of the price war and competition. When Netflix had announced its price cut in October 2004, its stock dropped, reaching a low of $9.50 per share. The stock wouldn't go back to its pre-announcement price until the middle of 2005.

NETFLIX AND WAL-MART
STRIKE A DEAL

As of 2010, according to a CNNMoney piece by Michael V. Copeland, a poster hanging in Netflix's headquarters showed the following image: a photo of a stock analyst, Michael Pachter, and the phrase "worthless piece of crap." A stock analyst's job is to study a company and make recommendations to investors about whether or not to buy that company's stock. The words on the poster were Pachter's opinion of Netflix's stock, which he voiced in January 2005. He was not alone among analysts who believed that Netflix's competition was going to put the company out of business.

A few months later, one company would quit its DVD subscription service, but that company was not Netflix. On May 19, 2005, Wal-Mart and Netflix announced jointly that Wal-Mart was ending its subscription service and would instead focus on selling DVDs. Wal-Mart and Netflix had struck an agreement. Wal-Mart would tell its soon-to-be former subscribers to join Netflix. Wal-Mart subscribers who switched to Netflix within a specified time period would get the same plan for the same price they had previously paid. In exchange, Netflix would tell its customers to go to Wal-Mart's Web site if they wanted to buy DVDs.

The first major threat to Netflix's life as a company was diffused when Wal-Mart and Netflix entered into an agreement. Wal-Mart ended its rental program and focused on selling DVDs instead.

Although Netflix had won a battle, Hastings acknowledged in an interview with *Inc.* magazine that there was still more to be done: "We're not celebrating victory at Netflix, though, because Wal-Mart never gave its best shot. Whereas Blockbuster is spending hundreds of millions of dollars, so when we beat them, it will be celebratory."

Blockbuster, for its part, issued its own press release that same day, enticing Wal-Mart and Netflix subscribers to switch to Blockbuster's service with the following offer:

two months free, a free DVD, and the opportunity to pay the same price they had been paying at Netflix and Wal-Mart for up to one year.

Netflix and Wal-Mart's deal would also cause a lawsuit to be brought against the companies. The plaintiffs, or those who brought the lawsuit, argued that the two companies worked together so that each could take over a market—DVD rentals for Netflix, DVD sales for Wal-Mart. Wal-Mart eventually decided to settle, or give money to the plaintiffs. Netflix decided to continue to fight the suit and would win in 2011.

Although Netflix would continue to compete with Blockbuster for years to come, its focus shifted to one of the things that was making the company successful: innovation.

CHAPTER 5

The Netflix Prize

"We're curious, really. To the tune of one million dollars." These were the first two sentences on the contest rules page for the Netflix Prize, a contest Netflix announced on October 2, 2006. It was looking for a way to improve its movie recommendation system, Cinematch, and decided the best way to do that was to start a contest open to everyone outside of Netflix, with a $1 million prize for the winner.

The idea for the Netflix Prize came from a contest called the Longitude Prize, put on by the British government 292 years ago. That contest challenged participants to develop a way to figure out a ship's longitude at sea. The winner used a unique method to achieve this result, and Netflix was hoping the participants of its own contest would find similarly unique ways to improve Netflix's movie recommendations.

To enter the contest, a participant or group of participants registered and received a data set, or a compilation

In addition to the $1 million cash prize, these medals were awarded to the members of the winning team in the Netflix Prize competition.

of information, to work with. The data set included one million rankings of 18,000 movie titles, made by 480,000 customers. The customers' identities were kept anonymous by replacing names with random ID numbers. The rankings, based on the 1 to 5 star ratings that customers would give to titles on the Web site, were made between October 1998 and December 2005. The only other information that came with the set was the date the anonymous customer ranked a title and the year the title came out.

Beat This Score

Between registering for the Netflix Prize and making it to $1 million was a series of challenges and incentives.

The qualifying test itself was split into two parts. The first was a qualifying quiz, which would help participants improve their system. The second part was the qualifying test, which Netflix would use to determine the winner. Netflix would post the results of a participant's or team's score on the qualifying quiz but keep the qualifying test results secret. It was like taking a test in which a teacher wouldn't reveal anyone's scores until someone got 100 percent.

Since the point of the contest was to be at least 10 percent more accurate than Cinematch in predicting ratings, all scores were relative to Cinematch's scores on the test. The scores were calculated according to a mathematical formula called root mean squared error, or RMSE. Netflix put Cinematch through the qualifying test and received a score of .9525. With RMSE, a lower score indicates better accuracy. The score for participants to match or beat was .8572.

The $1 million was not the only thing up for grabs. Since the contest was probably going to be a lengthy one, the Netflix Prize contest also gave out progress prizes. For every year the contest continued before a participant reached a score of .8572, Netflix would hand out $50,000 progress prizes to the participant that had improved the most that year, as long as there had been at least a 1 percent improvement over the previous year's best score. For the first year, the baseline was going to be the Cinematch score.

The results on the quiz scores were used to track progress. When a participant reached the qualifying score (.8572) on the quiz, Netflix would run the submission, called the prediction set, through the qualifying test. At that point, Netflix would inform all participants they had thirty days to submit their prediction sets, which it would also run through the test. The participant with the best score less than .8572 would be declared the winner. In the case of a tie, it would come down to who submitted first.

Along with the data set, participants received what Netflix called a qualifying test. This qualifying test contained over 2.8 million pairs of data: the pair was just a customer and a movie title. This is what contestants would use to measure their progress.

The pairs in the qualifying test were taken from customers already in the data set. The rankings for the customer/title pairs were kept secret from participants and represented the most recent rankings those customers had made. The rankings were essentially Netflix's answer sheet for figuring out a participant's score on the qualifying test, since it was the job of contest participants to figure out a system that would predict those rankings.

TEAMWORK

With a $1 million prize, it's not surprising that the Netflix Prize contest drew a lot of interest and a lot of participants. Within the first year of the contest, there were 2,550 teams with a combined total of 27,000 contestants from 161 countries.

Many teams made rapid initial progress. According to a paper by James Bennett and Stan Lanning, both of Netflix, by June 2007, 650 teams had better RMSE scores than Netflix, with 90 percent of those teams' scores being at least 5 percent better than Netflix's. If no team was going to reach the 10 percent goal that year, it was clear there would be a progress prizewinner.

On November 13, 2007, Netflix announced the first winners of the progress prize, going to a team that had submitted their prediction set half an hour before the progress prize deadline: KorBell, a team comprised of

Team Mergers

Although this was a contest, many of the teams discussed their progress and setbacks with each other, often through the forum on the Netflix Prize Web site. The Web site featured a leader board that posted the progress of the top teams. Very successful teams started to realize they were missing some small piece of the puzzle needed to put them over the top.

Part of figuring out a good algorithm involved figuring out how customers' thoughts and behaviors related to their ratings. One team, for example, was studying what happened when customers rated a lot of movies at once, while another team looked at how the day of the week during which customers made their ratings affected how highly they rated titles. Groups like these, coming from difference angles, realized they needed to combine their unique ideas, and mergers between teams started to take place.

When groups with very comprehensive algorithms joined with groups whose focus was more specified, the addition of those algorithms helped to push the scores up.

three coworkers from AT&T. Their winning submission was 8.43 percent better than Cinematch. As with the rules regarding the main prize, the team had to describe in writing and share with Netflix how their system worked.

With a first-year score of 8.43 percent, it would seem that reaching 10 percent wouldn't take too much longer, but it was those last couple of percentage points that proved hardest to attain.

As it turned out, the team that won the progress prize in the second year, in December 2008, BellKor in BigChaos, was one of those combined teams. If the name sounds vaguely familiar, it is because the team was a merger between KorBell, the previous year's winner, and a team that had become one of KorBell's main competitors, BigChaos. Their improvement percentage that year was 9.44 percent.

After submitting its winning score, BellKor in Big-Chaos would raise its score again, ever so slightly, to 9.56 percent. Progress at this point came more slowly. As Neil Hunt, Netflix's chief product officer, said in a press release after BellKor's newest score, "Hitting that last .44 percent is less of a dash to the finish line and more of a tough slog to the peak of Mt. Everest."

THE WINNER, BY A HAIR

It was BellKor in BigChaos that was the first to reach the 10 percent improvement score on the qualifying quiz, except

Reed Hastings and Netflix chief product officer, Neil Hunt, pose with the members of BellKor's Pragmatic Chaos—the team that won the Netflix Prize—during the awards ceremony in New York.

it was called BellKor's Pragmatic Chaos by then, having combined with a third team called Pragmatic Theory. This triggered the thirty-day period that all teams now had to submit their final prediction sets for the qualifying test. By that point, there were 40,000 teams representing 186 countries in the contest. Teams could keep working and submitting until July 26, 2009, and they did.

The winning score came during the last hour of the contest's lifespan, and two teams had it. BellKor's Pragmatic Chaos and the Ensemble, another merged team, both ended up with a final score of 10.06 percent improvement over Cinematch. The tiebreaker would come down to who submitted first.

BellKor's Pragmatic Chaos's final score was submitted with only twenty-four minutes left in the contest, but it was enough to win, beating out the Ensemble by less than half an hour. The race between the two was so tight, however, that it would take three weeks for the judges to review the results before they announced BellKor's Pragmatic Chaos as the winner.

When the seven members of the team collected their check at an awards ceremony on September 21, 2009, it was the first time all seven had met in person. The team had been working together remotely, spread across the United States, Austria, Canada, and Israel.

Neil Hunt, Netflix's chief product officer, has been working at Netflix since 1999. Reed Hastings has known Hunt for longer than that, since Hunt worked at Pure Software, Hastings's first company.

A NEW CONTEST

The same day the prizes were awarded to the contest winners, Hastings was ready to do it all again. Hastings announced a second Netflix contest, with another $1 million prize. The purpose of this contest was to go after the customers who rarely or never rated movies and figure out a way to improve the accuracy of suggestions for them. This time, not wanting to go through the drama of another multi-year contest, Hastings outlined the new contest's time parameters: $500,000 would go to the team with the best score at the end of six months, and an additional $500,000 would go to the team with the best score after eighteen months, with no specific minimum score.

This time, the data set the participants were to receive would include information about the still anonymous users, including age and zip codes of the users. This, as it would soon turn out, would get Hastings in trouble.

On December 19, 2009, a class-action lawsuit was filed against Netflix, alleging that Netflix had violated users' privacy by releasing data through the Netflix Prize contest. Netflix settled the suit, meaning that it agreed to pay money to the plaintiffs, or those who had brought the suit, instead of going to trial. This also meant the end for Netflix's new contest. On March 12, 2010, in a blog post on the Netflix Web site, Neil Hunt announced that Netflix was canceling its contest due to the settlement and talks with the Federal Trade Commission.

CHAPTER 6

Innovation and Expansion

At the same time that Netflix was seeking to make improvements to its internal recommendation system with the Netflix Prize, it was also beginning a period of major growth. This began with the introduction of a service that Reed Hastings had been waiting for practically from the moment he founded the company. Online video viewing had finally arrived at Netflix.

The new service was introduced on January 16, 2007. In order to monitor the service and fix any issues as they happened, Netflix instituted a slow rollout of the plan, meaning that it would add a specific amount of subscribers to the plan in January and continue to add subscribers until June, when all subscribers were expected to have the service.

Years ago, when Hastings was anticipating Internet-based movie viewing, the assumption was that viewers would download movies to view, meaning they would have to wait before the entire file was delivered to their computers before they could watch a movie. What Netflix ended up offering was movie streaming, which allowed viewers to watch a movie at the same time it was being sent to their computers. Netflix referred to this as immediate viewing, adding it to its Web site in a new "Watch Now" section.

Netflix added streaming to customers' already existing plans at no extra charge. The number of streaming hours customers could use was tied to the type of plan they had: six hours under the cheapest plan ($5.99) and eighteen under the most expensive (the $17.99 three-DVD unlimited plan). Unlike its DVDs, most of which were obtained by direct purchase or through revenue sharing, Netflix's video streaming offerings were obtained through licensing agreements with studios. Under this type of agreement, Netflix could offer titles for a specified amount of time and had to pay a royalty to the studio each time a movie was viewed.

When Netflix's streaming service was announced, Hastings reiterated in a press release the prediction made years ago that had led Netflix to that day: "We named our company Netflix in 1998 because we believed Internet-based movie rental represented the future, first as a means of improving service and selection, and then as a means of movie delivery."

Netflix was still counting on DVD rentals as its main source of revenue. DVDs had been such a small portion

Reed Hastings poses with a Roku box connected to a television. The Roku box was the first device created that made streaming Netflix through the television possible.

of video viewing when Netflix started and then became a dominant force, and Hastings believed that was the direction streaming would take. He explained during the streaming announcement: "While mainstream consumer adoption of online movie watching will take a number of years due to content and technology hurdles, the time is right for Netflix to take the first step." Interestingly, the number of initial titles available for streaming at the launch—one thousand—was about the same amount of DVD titles that Netflix had when it started its subscription service in 1999.

PARTNERSHIPS

The success of Netflix's streaming service rested on creating and maintaining key partnerships. The first of these partnerships involved Netflix's relationship with movie studios.

With DVDs, Netflix had a choice: revenue sharing or out-right purchase. The laws governing DVD rentals allowed Netflix to buy any DVD it wished and then rent that DVD to its customers. If a studio did not want to enter into a revenue-sharing agreement, Netflix could just buy that studio's DVD titles instead.

Streaming, however, did not fall under those rules. With streaming, studios were the ultimate gatekeepers. If Netflix wanted to show a title through instant streaming, it would have to enter a licensing agreement with the studio that owned that title. If the studio didn't want to enter a licensing agreement with Netflix, Netflix wouldn't be able to show titles from that studio. The ability of Netflix to expand the titles it offered through streaming depended on its success in arranging licensing agreements.

Netflix faced a similar situation when it came to its strategy of figuring out how to stream. When it introduced its streaming service, the only way to stream a movie was through the Internet on a PC, and a short time later, on a Mac. This was a good first step, but Netflix was also looking for ways to allow customers to watch streamed movies on a television screen, before the existence of televisions that could connect to the Internet internally.

One way Netflix did this was by partnering with device manufacturers, that is, the companies that had created machines such as TiVo, Blu-Ray, and Xbox, and set-top boxes such as Roku, which were made specifically

Strategies Take Time to Work

In Netflix's statements to its shareholders after opening in Canada, when Netflix referenced its international operations, it would state that it wasn't going to be making money there for some time. Why would Netflix take its business to other countries expecting to lose money? If you recall, it took Netflix five years to make its first profit. Before it did, it was spending a lot of money building up its company and trying to attract enough customers to cover the costs of those efforts. Once Netflix made its first profit, however, its revenue kept growing. What had begun as a five-year gamble turned into the largest Internet-based DVD rental and streaming company in the United States.

Netflix was hoping for the same type of scenario internationally. Even though Netflix was an established company when it entered into Canada, in many ways it operated, by necessity, as a start-up. Going into a new country required new licensing agreements, new Web sites, new staff, and new laws that Netflix needed to understand and follow. This time, however, instead of relying on investors and creditors to keep the company going, Netflix had the profit from its U.S. business to counter its international losses.

Canada served as Netflix's guinea pig for the international market. If Netflix did well in Canada, it would expand to other countries. To measure this, Netflix would look at how long it took its operations in Canada to make money. In its 2010 annual report to the SEC, Netflix noted that it felt Canada was doing well and could be profitable by 2011. This was enough to convince Netflix to expand into Latin America and the Caribbean (which it would in 2011) and the UK and Ireland (2012).

to allow streaming on televisions. Netflix made arrangements with these companies that allowed it to install software programs on their machines. When customers connected those devices to their televisions, they would be able to stream Netflix on their TV screens.

As with licensing agreements, Netflix's ability to do this depended on those companies continuing to allow Netflix to put (and upgrade) its software on their machines. For Netflix, maintaining good relationships with its partners became an integral part of its streaming success. It seemed to be working; by the end of 2008, Netflix had expanded its streaming options to twelve thousand titles and was looking to add even more.

This photo shows Netflix being streamed through a television connected to an Xbox 360 player, one of the many gaming consoles and device companies Netflix teamed up with to allow Netflix to stream on televisions.

For Hastings, 2007 also marked the beginning of a new role outside of Netflix. The Microsoft Corporation invited him to join its board of directors on March 28, 2007. The board, which previously consisted of nine people, added a tenth position, electing Hastings as the tenth member. The board of directors for a company is there to represent the company's stockholders and is responsible for many important decisions. For example, the board is responsible for hiring and firing a company's executives, or leaders, and it makes decisions about major company policies.

NETFLIX GOES GLOBAL

In 2010, for the first time, the number of movies and TV shows being viewed through streaming surpassed the number of titles being watched through DVD rentals. This, coupled with the fact that Netflix's device partnerships allowed customers to get video streaming in a variety of different ways, made 2010 a good time for Netflix to go international.

On September 22, 2010, Netflix made its debut in Canada. Not only did the launch represent Net-flix's first international venture, but it also marked the first streaming-only subscription plan that Netflix had ever offered. It created a single subscription plan in Canada, an unlimited streaming plan that would cost Canadians $7.99 a month.

The popularity of streaming allowed Netflix to expand into Canada and avoid extra expenses—including postage and the creation of new DVD distribution centers—that providing a DVD rental plan would have entailed.

This didn't, however, mean there weren't any extra expenses: Netflix would have to obtain separate licensing agreements for the movies it wanted to stream in Canada. Since Netflix wasn't as well known in Canada as in the

Reed Hastings announces the launch of Netflix's Canadian streaming service in Toronto, Canada. Appropriately enough, he stands in front of a large map of the country.

United States, it would also need to spend more money on marketing to make itself more of a household name.

BUSINESSPERSON OF THE YEAR

More than a decade of work turning a small dot-com into an international business put Reed Hastings on the cover of *Fortune* magazine in November 2010. Hastings had earned the title of *Fortune*'s Business Person of the Year for 2010, beating out forty-nine runners-up for the title.

That year had indeed been a good one for Hastings. In addition to an expansion into Canada, Netflix had gotten twenty million subscribers by December 2010. What made this particularly impressive was the rate at which Netflix had grown its subscribers in the previous years. By the end of 2009, Netflix had about 12.3 million subscribers. This represented a 63.1 percent increase between 2009 and 2010. The previous year, in 2008, Netflix had about 9.4 million subscribers, which meant the increase in subscribers from 2008 to 2009 had been 30.6 percent, or just under half the 2009–2010 increase. It had taken Netflix four years since the launch of its subscription service to get to one million subscribers, in 2003. Since 2003, it had taken Netflix seven years to reach twenty million.

In 2011, the accomplishments for Hastings and Netflix continued to pile up. On June 23, 2011, he added to his

Netflix Customer Service

One of the reasons why Netflix was able to attract, and more important, retain so many subscribers was because of its well-regarded customer service. The first sentence in Hastings's letter to shareholders in 2007 read, "Each year since we invented online DVD rental in 1999, Netflix has focused on understanding the preferences of our subscribers and on improving the customer experience," demonstrating how important he believed customer satisfaction to be to the success of the business.

Many of Netflix's innovations, from its Cinematch technology and Netflix Prize to its no-late-fee, subscription-based plans, were implemented with an eye toward improving upon the customer experience. Netflix's customer service is open twenty-four hours a day, seven days a week, and is based in the United States.

Netflix consistently rated high in customer service satisfaction surveys. Through 2010, for example, it had taken the number one spot six years in a row in a customer satisfaction survey of top Internet companies conducted by ForeSee, a company that focuses on studying customer service.

technology company board experience by being appointed to Facebook's board of directors.

On July 11, 2011, Netflix's stock also reached a milestone: its shares reached an all-time high of $304.79. There seemed to be nothing but good news for the company for the near future, but an ill-planned announcement was about to change that.

CHAPTER 7

"I Messed Up"

T he day after its stock reached an all-time high, Netflix delivered an important announcement: it was splitting up its streaming and DVD-by-mail service.

In a July 12 blog post on the Netflix blog detailing the change, Netflix's vice president of marketing, Jessie Becker, wrote that because streaming was more popular than DVD rentals, Netflix wanted to place its focus there, which was the reason why Netflix was splitting up the services.

The new plans announced on July 2011 included a one-DVD-at-a-time unlimited plan for $7.99 and a two-DVD-at-a-time unlimited plan for $11.99. Netflix kept its $7.99-a-month unlimited streaming plan—which it had introduced in November 2010—as it was. Streaming would no longer be included with the DVD plans, so if customers wanted both unlimited steaming and DVDs, they would have to sign up for both plans. In this way, a one-DVD plan with unlimited streaming would now cost customers $15.98, instead of the $9.99 they had been

A laptop is open to Netflix's Web site. On the site, Netflix's $7.99 plan for unlimited streaming is being advertised, demonstrating Netflix's focus on streaming over its DVD rental portion of the business.

paying. The plan for existing members would take effect on September 1, 2011.

The response to this news was immediate. The post on the Netflix blog that detailed the plan received over twelve thousand comments, many of which expressed customers' anger or disappointment with the plans, or announced their intentions to cancel their subscriptions.

Initially, Hastings didn't appear overly concerned. According to Brian Stelter in the *New York Times*, Hastings acknowledged that he expected some discontent and loss of subscribers, but he didn't believe the loss would be too significant, speculating that the number of subscribers lost would be "a few."

As it would turn out, Hastings had underestimated just how upset subscribers were by the plan changes. As Netflix subscribers started to cancel their accounts, it became clear that it was going to be a lot more than a few customers.

A BOTCHED APOLOGY

On September 18, 2011, in a post entitled "An Explanation and Some Reflections," Reed Hastings offered up an apology to Netflix customers on the Netflix blog. Hastings acknowledged that many of the responses Netflix received about the changes reflected customers' unhappiness with how it handled the announcement.

In the subsequent explanation he offered, Hastings wrote that he was worried, as streaming became more popular, that Netflix wouldn't be as good at streaming as it was with its DVD service and felt a need to act quickly to ensure that the company would be on top of streaming. Hastings worried about the repercussions of not effectively adapting new technologies like streaming quickly enough.

What he was apologizing for, according to the post, was not the plan and price changes, but for failing to communicate with customers about the changes and explain the purpose of those changes.

Reed Hastings is pictured here after his attempt to apologize when his unpopular price hike announcement was met with as much resistance as the announcement itself.

The reason the services should be separated, Hastings went on to explain, was that he felt that DVD by mail and streaming had different challenges and requirements.

As a result, Hastings announced in his apology that he was literally turning DVD by mail and streaming into two different companies. DVDs would still arrive in their red envelopes, Hastings said, but the envelopes were going to read "Qwikster," Hastings's name for the new DVD-by-mail business. The streaming service would keep Netflix as its name. The two different services would have separate Web sites, and, if customers wanted both services, they would have to create two separate accounts, one for each company.

This time around, Hastings's post received over twenty-seven thousand mainly unhappy comments. The response was enough to convince Hastings that the Qwikster/Netflix split was a bad idea. On Monday, October 10, 2011, Hastings made another post to the Netflix blog, announcing that he wasn't going forward with Qwikster; DVD rentals and streaming would both stay on Netflix.

AFTERMATH

It would take a few months for the effects of Hastings's decisions to really be felt. While customer reactions were the first outward sign of how bad a decision this would

Customers Respond

As of July 2012, the combined responses to Netflix's announcement of separate prices for DVD-by-mail and subscription plans and to Hastings's apology generated over thirty-nine thousand comments. To give an idea of how unusual this was, the blog post that generated the next highest amount of responses in September 2011 had just under two hundred comments. Many comments showed displeasure at the new decisions in different ways:

- Some customers responded by simply stating that they were planning to cancel their subscriptions.
- Others stated that not only were they going to cancel, they were going to tell everyone they knew to cancel as well.
- Some customers specified which of Netflix's competitors they were planning to switch to, such as Hulu and Redbox.
- Some thought the idea of having two separate services under two different companies inconvenient or a bad business idea.
- Some questioned the timing of the decision, believing that the lack of serious competition was the reason Netflix raised its prices.

- Some customers were unhappy with the tone of the letter, writing that it didn't feel like a real apology.
- Some commenters described feeling betrayed by the new plans and organizational changes.

The comments weren't all completely negative; there were customers who posted comments defending the change, writing that the plans justified higher prices.

turn out to be for the company, more concrete, number-driven evidence soon appeared.

The loss of subscribers, for one, was more than Hastings had anticipated. By October 24, 2011, when Netflix sent out its quarterly report, the report detailed just how much damage had been done: Netflix had lost 800,000 subscribers between June 30, 2011, and September 30, 2011.

Netflix's membership count wasn't the only thing that started to drop. Its stock price, which had never looked better than in July, started to fall. It was a slow slide until September 15, 2011, when, in a letter to shareholders, Hastings announced that Netflix was expecting to lose subscribers in the coming months. By the end of the day, shares of Netflix were going for $169.25, down from the previous day's price of $208.75, a difference of $39.50. By the end of September, Netflix's stock was down to $113.27 a share. Another large drop happened in late October 2011. On October 25, the day after the quarterly report came out detailing how many subscribers Netflix had lost, its stock dropped to $77.37 from the previous day's $118.84. The lowest point, however, wouldn't come until the next month, on November 25, 2011, when the stock fell to $63.86. The last time the stock had been that low was in February 2010, when Netflix's stock was beginning it climb toward $300.

Hastings's salary was also cut. For 2012, Hastings would be earning $2 million, $1.5 million less than his previous year's salary of $3.5 million.

The pain wasn't only financial. When Hastings wrote the Qwikster post, he included a video he made with the man who was supposed to be the new CEO of Qwikster, Andy Rendich. The video became popular, but not in a way that Hastings would have preferred. Hastings had wanted the video to be casual, unrehearsed, and low tech, and he succeeded on that front. It was of just him and Rendich, sitting outside at a table in Netflix's courtyard. Hastings was dressed in a teal button-down shirt, and Rendich in a gray one. At times, the video would cut off the top of their heads, and background noise hummed the whole time, like the sound of rushing water. It wasn't long before parodies of the video started appearing, including ones made

Life Outside of Netflix

Throughout the Qwikster fiasco, Hastings continued his interest and longtime involvement with education projects. In addition to serving on the board of directors for two tech companies, Hastings held positions on the boards of education-related organizations. Hastings had a strong interest in charter schools, which was evident since at least his days as president of the California State Board of Education. In 2007, he had begun serving on the board of the KIPP Foundation, which supports the work of the KIPP schools, one of the most successful groups of charter schools in the country. The following year, he joined the board of the California Charter School Association.

Two years later, in 2010, Hastings was able to combine his belief in the potential of technology and his interest in education when he worked with an organization called the Charter School Growth Fund to purchase a company called DreamBox Learning. DreamBox Learning creates interactive, online math lessons for children that are individually tailored to each child who uses them.

In 2011, Hastings's education experience was acknowledged by Secretary of Education Arne Duncan when he appointed Hastings to the newly created Equity and Excellence Commission. The Equity and Excellence Commission's job is to examine spending on schools and figure out ways to make that spending more equal, something that Hastings has some background in with his work on the Proposition 39 campaign.

by the sketch comedy show *Saturday Night Live* and comedian Conan O'Brien.

LESSONS LEARNED

What the Qwikster debacle demonstrated was that no company, no matter how successful or popular, is impervious to making mistakes in judgment and that those mistakes can do a lot of damage in a short amount of time.

Hubris is an idea that comes from ancient Greece and expresses the idea of excessive pride. In Greek plays, a person with too much hubris often experiences a tragic turn of fate as the result of that hubris. In an interview in *Vanity Fair*, Hastings acknowledged his hubris caused Netflix's twist of luck, saying he was "guilty of overconfidence."

Hastings said this was also the reason why he hadn't wanted to listen to anyone but himself about this idea; small warning signs had been there, which he had

The launch page for Qwikster, announcing its impending arrival. Qwikster never arrived; the planned Netflix DVD spinoff that was Qwikster was scrapped after overwhelming customer unhappiness with this plan.

dismissed. A *New York Times* article described how Hastings had told his friend about the Qwikster plans before they had happened, while he and his friend were hanging out in a hot tub. The friend didn't like the plan, telling Hastings it would be annoying for customers to handle two accounts. Hastings thought he knew better than his friend and dismissed his friend's feedback. What ended up happening, Hastings said in *Vanity Fair*, was that "Qwikster became the symbol of Netflix not listening."

While acknowledging his mistakes, Hastings seemed intent on not dwelling too much on what had happened. Instead, his focus shifted to making improvements to earn back the trust of customers. One of the main ways Hasting wanted to accomplish this was by focusing on expanding streaming options for Netflix customers.

CHAPTER 8

The Future Arrived. Now What?

Over a decade ago, when Reed Hastings was starting Netflix, he imagined a future for his DVD-by-mail business that was very different from what the company was at its beginning. Though it wasn't exactly as he had pictured it—viewers now stream instead of download—in the big picture, his instincts about what lay ahead led him and his company to that future.

On January 3, 2011, Netflix made an announcement that formed the beginning of a new vision and direction for the company. It announced that it was premiering an original series, *Lilyhammer*. The show, featuring a mobster under witness protection who moves to Norway, represented Netflix's first effort to create its own television programming. The company that made its money bringing thousands of episodes of TV shows to subscribers was starting to create some of its own.

When *Lilyhammer* premiered on Netflix on February 6, 2012, it did so in a way unusual for how TV shows

Steve Van Zandt, star of Netflix's first original program, *Lilyhammer*, poses with wife Maureen Van Zandt at the show's premiere. Also pictured are former *Sopranos* castmates Vincent Pastore, Steve Schirripa, and Tony Sirico.

were typically presented. Instead of airing one episode at a time, leaving viewers waiting in anticipation of the following week's episode, Netflix provided all eight episodes of the first season that same day.

While *Lilyhammer* was the first original show to come out on Netflix, it was not the first to be announced. In November 2011, Netflix had announced that in 2013 it would be showing the new season of the popular, previously canceled show *Arrested Development*. Announcements for other new shows followed, for a total

Changing How Television Is Done

Netflix's entrance as a home for original content has the potential to change how television is done, both for the people who provide programming and those who create it.

One important change Netflix made when it premiered *Lilyhammer* was to have the entire season available at once. It plans to continue this strategy. That decision has important implications for the creators of those shows. The writers for *Arrested Development*, for example, decided to change the direction of the new season as a result. In the seasons before its cancellation, *Arrested Development* was filled with many clever story lines and jokes that sometimes required viewers to re-watch an episode to figure out what they missed the first time. Because all the new season's episodes would be available at the same time, the show's creators planned to fill the show with even more nuances and hidden references, since viewers will have the ability to re-watch episodes and put it together all at once.

Thanks to Cinematch, Netflix can predict the types of TV shows that will be popular with subscribers and use that information when choosing its original programming.

Netflix is free from many of the constraints of network and cable TV channels. With no specific airdates for its episodes, Netflix doesn't have to worry about competing for viewers of other shows in the same time slot—there is no time slot.

Netflix is also an appealing place for show creators because it gives their shows time and space to grow. Netflix purchased two seasons of *House of Cards*, meaning it will pay to produce two seasons' worth of episodes. Network and cable television will often pay for a few episodes to be produced, and if a show doesn't do well enough during those first few episodes, the show will be canceled. Shows on Netflix will have more time to grow their audience.

This is just what happened to *Arrested Development*. The cable channel Showtime was also interested in airing the new season of *Arrested Development*. One of the reasons Mitch Hurwitz, the show's creator, decided to go with Netflix was because Netflix had, through streaming old seasons, created many new fans of the show: "It's been like putting jokes in a bottle and then having them come back years later to say, 'Ha ha,'" he said in a *New York* magazine Vulture post.

of four new shows Netflix will premiere in 2013. In addition to *Arrested Development*, the other shows are *House of Cards*, a political thriller starring Kevin Spacey; *Hemlock Grove*, a murder-mystery horror series; and *Orange Is the New Black*, a comedy set in a women's prison.

Netflix's success lies in getting more and more subscribers to sign up for the service. Before it introduced original programming, the way it got more subscribers was to constantly improve its streaming offerings. However, as companies old and new began to try out their own streaming services, the competition to get exclusive

The cast of *Arrested Development*, which is being revived by Netflix. Pictured clockwise from back: Will Arnett, Portia de Rossi, David Cross, Tony Hale, Jason Bateman, Jeffrey Tambor, Jessica Walter, Alia Shawkat, and Michael Cera.

licensing deals with studios and distributors ramped up. For a movie studio or distributor, having so many companies hungry for its titles gives it an incentive to up its prices and demands.

With original programming, Netflix is hoping to attract and keep subscribers in a new way. In an interview with Nick Summers in *Newsweek*, Hastings said of the effort, "When we started it a year ago, we viewed it as a strategic experiment. Now we view it as a strategic direction."

NEW CHALLENGES

Although Blockbuster still manages to hang on, Netflix came out ahead in the DVD wars, maintaining its position as the largest DVD-by-mail company in the United States. As DVDs began their slow decline, Netflix was prepared, having gotten into streaming long before streaming became the preferred option for viewing movies and TV shows.

With DVDs by mail, Netflix had gotten a head start on its competitors, spending years on securing licensing agreements and building up its library. With streaming, however, the concept of a library of titles is a less stable, less definite one. With streaming, if a licensing agreement expires and a studio doesn't want to renew, the titles that Netflix had spent time and money to obtain disappear from menus and queues as if they had never existed. It's easier for others to catch up.

A crowd in front of a Redbox kiosk waits to rent or return movies. Redbox, one of Netflix's competitors, allows renters to pick up and return movies from the kiosks without a membership.

The Doctrine of Net Neutrality

At the core of Netflix's fight over Internet broadband limits with cable companies like Comcast is the idea of net neutrality and whether it applies to data caps. Net neutrality is the principle that the Internet should serve as a neutral transmitter of information.

The Federal Communication Commission (FCC) is the government organization in charge of overseeing communications—i.e., radio, television, wire, satellite, and cable—in the United States. On November 20, 2011, the FCC came out with a set of guidelines for net neutrality, or what it calls the "open Internet." The report, "The Open Internet Report and Order," highlights three rules necessary for an open Internet:

- Transparency: Companies that provide Internet should make available information about themselves and their services, including prices and performance.
- No blocking: An Internet provider cannot choose to block the Web site of a company it doesn't like or is in competition with, or any site or service for any reason other than a site being illegal.

- No unreasonable discrimination: An Internet provider must allow all sites to run in the same way. It can't allow certain sites to run faster or slower than other sites.

Netflix's self-reported list of competitors includes companies offering entertainment services over a variety of formats: Blockbuster and Redbox, which both offer vending-machine–style DVD rentals; Amazon.com Prime and Hulu Plus, two streaming services; and what Netflix calls multichannel video programming distributors, which include HBO GO and Showtime Anytime. In its 2011 annual report to the SEC, Netflix indicated that it wasn't too worried about competition from Hulu because customers would be subject to watching commercials, even through its paying service. Netflix felt that its advantage came in providing commercial-free viewing. Its main concerns were with HBO GO and Showtime Anytime, which allowed users who were subscribers to those cable channels to watch current and past seasons of shows on multiple devices, including computers and tablets.

During the winter of the following year, a new service came on the scene that had the potential not only to compete with Netflix but also to create an uneven playing field. On February 21, 2012, Comcast—a cable television,

Internet, and telephone service provider—announced a new streaming service called Xfinity Streampix. At that point in time, Comcast had in place an Internet usage cap for its customers—users could not use more than 250 GB of Internet data per month. On April 15, Reed Hastings posted on his Facebook page that he had streamed Netflix, HBO GO, Hulu, and Xfinity through his Xbox. Hastings, a Comcast customer, noticed that all services with the exception of Xfinity added to his Internet data usage. This in effect gave Comcast customers an extra incentive to choose Xfinity over the other services. In the same post,

David Hyman, a lawyer representing Netflix, speaks on July 27, 2012, at the House of Representatives Subcommittee on Energy and Technology and argues for legislation regulating how companies cap their data.

Hastings accused Comcast of violating net neutrality by not subjecting Xfinity to the data cap the other services had to contend with.

Hastings's post received a lot of attention, culminating on June 27, 2012, in a U.S. House of Representatives hearing. Netflix testified at the hearing, put on by the Subcommittee on Communications and Technology, to argue for new rules to prevent companies like Comcast from putting limits on how much Internet data its customers could use.

THE NUMBERS NOW

Just as Netflix was starting to make a slow recovery from its subscriber and stock loss of 2011, it came out with its 2012 second-quarter earnings report to shareholders on July 24, 2012. The news was mixed.

Netflix had managed to pick up subscribers in domestic and international streaming, and had 23.9 million domestic and 3.6 million international subscribers by June 30, 2012. The number of subscribers to the DVD plans, however, dropped, and Netflix had 9.24 million DVD subscribers at the end of June 2012.

Netflix also made a profit of $6.2 million after having lost money in the first three months of the year.

In its report, Netflix stated that it was happy with the way things were going with its international services

Reed Hastings scrolls through some movie choices on the Netflix Web site in London at the launch of Netflix's service for Ireland and the United Kingdom.

and that, as a result, it was planning to offer Netflix in another international market.

None of this seemed to make investors happy, however, and the day after Netflix released its report, its stock dropped to $60.28 a share, which represented a $20 fall from July 24, 2012, when Netflix stock was $80.39 a share.

The problem for investors was that even though Netflix had improved, it hadn't improved enough. Netflix was gaining new subscribers at a much lower rate than the previous year. The fact that Netflix lost DVD subscribers was problematic for investors; the company made more money off of its DVD customers because expensive licensing agreements made streaming subscribers more expensive for Netflix.

A year after its fall from grace, Netflix is trying to rebuild its reputation. For Hastings, the way to accomplish this is to focus on Netflix's future. That future, according to Hastings in the report, is in continuing to expand Netflix's influence internationally and really build Netflix up as a global company. The future also lies, potentially, in its original programming, and 2013 will be the year that can demonstrate how successful Netflix will be in that arena.

Some investors and critics may be pessimistic about Netflix's future, but they've been wrong before and Reed Hastings has the poster to prove it.

Fact Sheet on
REED HASTINGS

Full Name: Wilmot Reed Hastings, Jr.

Nickname: Reed Hastings

Date of Birth: October 8, 1960

Birthplace: Belmont, Massachusetts

Current Residence: California

Salary: $500,000

Salary with Stock Options: $2,000,0000

Marital Status: Married

Children: Two sons

High School: Buckingham Browne & Nichols

Colleges Attended: Bowdoin College, BA 1983
Stanford University, MSCS 1988

First Company: Pure Atria Software

Corporate Board Memberships: Microsoft (2007–Present), Facebook (2011–Present)

Nonprofit Board Memberships: KIPP (2007–Present), California Charter Schools Association (2008–Present), Dreambox (2010–Present)

Government Experience: California State Board of Education (2000–2004), president (2001–2004); commission member, U.S. Department of Education Equity and Excellence Commission (2011–Present)

Philanthropic Interests: Education, charter schools

Volunteer Experience: Peace Corps volunteer, 1983–1985

Fact Sheet on

NETFLIX

Date Incorporated: August 29, 1997

Founded By: Reed Hastings and Marc Randolph

CEO: Reed Hastings

Headquarters: 100 Winchester Circle
Los Gatos, CA 95032

Number of Employees: 2,348 (as of December 31, 2011)

Phone: (408) 540-3700

Web Site: www.netflix.com

Annual Revenue (2011): $3,204,577,000

Annual Domestic Revenue (2011): $3,121,727,000

Annual International Revenue (2011): $82,850,000

Average Monthly Revenue per Paying Subscriber (2011): $11.84

Net Worth (2011): $642,810,000

Number of Subscribers (2011): 26,253,000

Number of Domestic Streaming Subscribers (2011): 21,671,000

Number of International Streaming Subscribers (2011): 1,858,000

Number of DVD Subscribers (2011): 11,165,000

Number of New Subscribers (2011): 6,243,000

Select List of Devices and Platforms Netflix Is Available on: Xbox 360, Nintendo Wii, Sony PlayStation 3, iPhone, iPad, Android

Date of Initial Public Offering: May 22, 2002

Stock Exchange Symbol: NFLX

Trades on: NASDAQ

Share Price: $56.85 (as of July 31, 2012)

Regions of Operation: United States, Canada, Latin America and the Caribbean, UK, Ireland

Services: Domestic streaming, international streaming, domestic DVD by mail

Timeline

October 8, 1960 Reed Hastings is born in Boston, Massachusetts.

1983 Reed Hastings graduates from Bowdoin with a B.A. in math.

1983–1985 Reed Hastings serves in the Peace Corps as a math teacher in Swaziland.

1988 Reed Hastings graduates from Stanford University with an MSCS in artificial intelligence.

1991 Reed Hastings founds and serves as CEO of Pure Software.

1997 Reed Hastings sells Pure Atria.

August 1997 Reed Hastings founds Netflix with partner Marc Randolph.

September 1998 Reed Hastings becomes CEO of Netflix.

1999 Netflix launches its subscription service, allowing customers to keep DVDs for as long as they like with no late fees.

2000 Netflix debuts Cinematch, its movie recommendation technology; Reed Hastings is appointed to the California State Board of Education.

May 2002 Netflix makes its stock market debut, trading as NFLX on Nasdaq.

June 2003 Netflix patents its subscription model.

October 2006 Netflix announces the Netflix Prize, a contest that will award $1 million to the person or team that can improve upon Netflix's recommendation system by 10 percent.

January 2007 Netflix begins its Internet streaming service.

March 2007 Reed Hastings is appointed to Microsoft's board of directors.

2008 Reed Hastings is appointed to the board of the California Charter School Association.

2009 Netflix announces BellKor's Pragmatic Chaos as the winner of the $1 million Netflix Prize; Netflix announces a new contest.

December 2009 A class-action lawsuit is brought against Netflix, alleging that the Netflix Prize violated data privacy.

March 2010 Netflix cancels the second contest.

September 2010 Netflix begins international service with the launch of streaming in Canada.

November 2010 Reed Hastings is named *Fortune*'s Businessperson of the Year for 2010.

2011 Netflix launches its streaming service in Latin America and the Caribbean.

June 2011 Reed Hastings is appointed to Facebook's board of directors.

July 2011 Netflix splits up its streaming and DVD-by-mail services, charging separate prices for each.

September 2011 Reed Hastings announces that Netflix's DVD-by-mail service is being spun off into a new company called Qwikster; Hastings posts an apology on Netflix's blog site, following the backlash surrounding Netflix's decision to split its streaming and DVD by mail services.

October 2011 Reed Hastings announces that he is cancelling plans to launch Qwikster.

November 2011 Netflix stocks drop to a then all-time low of $62 per share.

February 2012 Netflix premieres its first original show, *Lilyhammer*.

2012 Netflix expands its streaming service to the UK and Ireland.

June 2012 Hastings appears before the U.S. House Communications and Technology Subcommittee to argue against data limits on broadband service.

Glossary

acquisition Something that is obtained through purchase or by other means.

algorithm A series of steps used to solve a problem or complete a task.

baseline A measurement that other measurements are compared against.

class action A type of lawsuit brought by a large group of people with the same complaint.

compliance The act of going along with a rule or law.

criteria A set of standards used to judge or measure something.

deference Respecting or following someone else's rules.

domestic Pertaining to something that happens in the United States.

electronic commerce/e-commerce Business involving buying or selling done over the Internet.

fiasco Something that is a total failure.

fiscal year A twelve-month period of time that companies use to measure their financial status. Does not necessarily go from January to December.

impervious Something that is not affected or influenced by anything.

incentive Something such as an award that motivates someone to take action or perform better.

intangible Something that cannot be touched because it lacks a physical form.

investor Someone who put money into something in the hopes of making more money than was put in.

leverage To use an advantage or an item to achieve a specific result.

licensing agreement An agreement that allows someone to use intellectual property or something that is copyrighted or trademarked.

market A place to buy and sell goods, or the buying and selling of a specific type of thing.

niche A specific portion of a market.

parameter A set boundary or a guideline.

patent Protection given by the government for intellectual property.

queue An ordered list of items; a line.

revenue The amount of money made by a company.

royalty A specific amount of money paid to the owner of a patent, trademark, or copyright.

stockholder/shareholder Someone who owns shares or stock in a company.

stock market A market where stocks are bought and sold.

transparency In business, the condition of allowing information to be open, easily visible, and understood.

viable Able to be done or realized.

For More Information

Electronic Frontier Foundation (EFF)

454 Shotwell Street

San Francisco, CA 94110

(415) 436-9333

Web site: http://www.eff.org

The Electronic Frontier Foundation is an organization that advocates for and protects Internet rights, and provides information and background about its campaigns.

National Alliance for Public Charter Schools

1101 15th Street NW, Suite 1010

Washington, DC 20005

(202) 289-2700

Web site: http://www.publiccharters.org

The National Alliance for Public Charter Schools provides statistics and information on charter schools in the United States.

National Film Board of Canada

Norman McLaren Building

3155 Côte de Liesse Road
Montreal, QC H4N 2N4
Canada
(514) 283-9000
Web site: http://www.nfb.ca/education
The National Film Board of Canada provides access to edu-
    cational films, as well as resources on digital education.

The Paley Center for Media
25 West 52nd Street
New York, NY 10019
(212) 621-6600
Web site: http://www.paleycenter.org
The Paley Center for Media provides information on the
    history of radio and television, including a database
    of television programs and features on topics such as
    the civil rights movement and media history.

Society of Internet Professionals
120 Carlton Street, Suite 305
Toronto, ON M5A 4K2
Canada
(416) 891-4937
Web site: http://www.sipgroup.org
The Society of Internet Professionals provides informa-
    tion and links to Internet-related topics such as social
    networking and Internet security.

U.S. Internet Industry Association
P.O. Box 302
Luray, VA 22834
(540) 742-1928
Web site: http://usiia-net.org/contact.htm
The U.S. Internet Industry Association provides publica-
    tions on Internet and e-commerce topics, as well as
    links to government sites that pertain to Internet-
    related issues.

U.S. Securities and Exchange Commission (SEC)
100 F Street NE
Washington, DC 20549
(202) 942-8088
Web site: http://www.sec.gov
The SEC protects investors and regulates the stock
    market. Its Web site provides information on pub-
    lic companies and a searchable database of their
    documents.

WEB SITES

Due to the changing nature of Internet links, Rosen Publishing has developed an online list of Web sites related
to the subject of this book. This site is updated regularly.
Please use this link to access the list:

http://www.rosenlinks.com/IBIO/Net

For Further Reading

Blum, Andrew. *Tubes: A Journey to the Center of the Internet.* New York, NY: Ecco, 2012.

Bourque, Peter. *Tarnished Ivory: Reflections on Peace Corps and Beyond.* Bloomington, IN: Xlibris, 2011.

Condie, Ally. *Matched.* New York, NY: Dutton, 2010.

Decherney, Peter. *Hollywood's Copyright Wars: From Edison to the Internet.* New York, NY: Columbia University Press, 2012.

Doctorow, Cory. *Little Brother.* New York, NY: Tor, 2008.

Dyson, George. *Turing's Cathedral: The Origins of the Digital Universe.* New York, NY: Pantheon Books, 2012.

Epstein, Edward Jay. *The Hollywood Economist: The Hidden Financial Reality Behind the Movies.* Brooklyn, NY: Melville House Publishing, 2010.

Espejo, Roman, ed. *Should the Internet Be Free?* (At Issue). Farmington Hills, MI: Greenhaven Press, 2010.

Falkner, Brian. *The Tomorrow Code.* New York, NY: Random House Children's Books, 2008.

Furgang, Kathy. *How the Stock Market Works.* New York, NY: Rosen Publishing Group, 2010.

Greenberg, Joshua M. *From Betamax to Blockbuster: Video Stores and the Invention of Movies on Video*

(Inside Technology). Cambridge, Massachusetts: MIT Press, 2008.

Howe, Jeff. *Crowdsourcing: Why the Power of the Crowd Is Driving the Future of Business*. New York, NY: Three Rivers Press, 2009.

Jinks, Catherine. *Evil Genius*. Orlando, FL: Harcourt, 2007.

Johnson, Steve. *Where Good Ideas Come From: The Natural History of Innovation*. New York, NY: Riverhead, 2010.

Kirk, Amanda. *Field Guides to Finding a New Career: Internet and Media*. New York, NY: Ferguson, 2011.

Lewis, Michael. *Panic: The Story of Modern Financial Insanity*. New York, NY: W. W. Norton, 2009.

MacCormick, John. *Nine Algorithms That Changed the Future: The Ingenious Ideas That Drive Today's Computers*. Princeton, NJ: Princeton University Press, 2012.

Mathews, Jay. *Work Hard. Be Nice: How Two Inspired Teachers Created the Most Promising Schools in America*. Chapel Hill, NC: Algonquin Books, 2009.

Plotkin, Robert. *Computers and Creativity*. New York, NY: Facts On File, 2012.

Rao, Arun, and Piero Scaruffi. *A History of Silicon Valley; The Greatest Creation of Wealth in the History of the Planet*. La Jolla, CA: Omniware, 2011.

Roman, Rick. *I'm a Shareholder Kit: The Basics About Stocks – For Kids/Teens*. 3rd ed. Gilbert, AZ: Leading Edge Gifts LLC, 2012.

Rose, Frank. *The Art of Immersion: How the Digital Generation Is Remaking Hollywood, Madison Avenue, and the Way We Tell Stories.* New York, NY: Norton & Company, 2011.

Rushkoff, Douglas. *Program or Be Programmed: Ten Commands for a Digital Age.* Berkeley, CA: Soft Skull Press, 2011.

Sacks, Mike. *And Here's the Kicker: Conversations with 21 Top Humor Writers on Their Craft.* Cincinnati, OH: Writer's Digest Books, 2009.

Vance, Ashlee. *Geek Silicon Valley: The Inside Guide to Palo Alto, Stanford, Menlo Park, Mountain View, Santa Clara, Sunnyvale, San Jose, San Francisco.* Kearney, NE: Morris Book Publishing, 2007.

Wu, Tim. *The Master Switch: The Rise and Fall of Information Empires.* New York, NY: Vintage Books, 2011.

Bibliography

Adalian, Josef. "Mitch Hurwitz Talks Arrested Development 2.0." Vulture.com, May 17, 2012. Retrieved July 20, 2012 (http://www.vulture .com/2012/04/mitch-hurwitz-talks-arrested -development-20.html).

Bennett, James, and Stan Lanning. "The Netflix Prize." Paper presented at the proceedings of KDD Cup and Workshop 2007, San Jose, California, August 12, 2007. Retrieved July 20, 2012 (http://www.cs.uic .edu/~liub/KDD-cup-2007/proceedings.html).

Cohan, William D. "Seeing Red." *Vanity Fair*, February 22, 2012. Retrieved July 20, 2012 (http://www .vanityfair.com/business/2012/02/netflix-201202).

Conlin, Michelle. "Netflix to the Max." *Bloomberg Businessweek*, September 23, 2007. Retrieved July 20, 2012 (http://www.businessweek.com /stories/2007-09-23/netflix-flex-to-the-max).

Copeland, Michael V. "Reed Hastings: Leader of the Pack." *Fortune*, November 18, 2010. Retrieved July 20, 2012 (http://tech.fortune.cnn.com/2010/11/18 /reed-hastings-leader-of-the-pack).

Gelsi, Steve. "Netflix Eyes Digital Future." MarketWatch .com, June 19, 2002. Retrieved June 1, 2012 (http:// www.marketwatch.com/story/netflix-founder-touts -future-role-in-digital-movies?pagenumber=1).

Hastings, Reed. "An Explanation and Some Reflections."
Netflix US & Canada Blog, September 18, 2011.
Retrieved July 20, 2012 (http://blog.netflix.com
/2011/09/explanation-and-some-reflections.html).

Hastings, Reed, as told to Amy Zipkins. "Out of Africa,
Onto the Web." *New York Times*, December 17, 2006.
Retrieved July 20, 2012 (http://www.nytimes.com
/2006/12/17/jobs/17boss.html?_r=2).

Hastings, Reed, as told to Patrick J. Sauer. "How I Did
It: Reed Hastings, Netflix." *Inc.*, December 1, 2005.
Retrieved July 20, 2012 (http://www.inc.com/magazine
/20051201/qa-hastings.html).

Hopkins, Jim. "'Charismatic' Founder Keeps Netflix Adapting."
USA Today, April 23, 2006. Retrieved July 20, 2012
(http://www.usatoday.com/money/companies
/management/2006-04-23-exec-ceo-profile-netflix_x.htm).

Mainelli, Tom. "Three Minutes with Netflix CEO Reed
Hastings." *PCWorld*, June 8, 2001. Retrieved July 20,
2012 (http://www.pcworld.com/article/51463/three
_minutes_with_netflix_ceo_reed_hastings.html).

Netflix, Inc. "Financial Statements." ir.netflix.com, 2002–
2012. Retrieved June 19, 2012 (http://ir.netflix.com
/financials.cfm?CategoryID=154&SortOrder=FileD
ate%20Descending&Year=&PageNum=1).

Netflix, Inc. "Netflix Inc. (NFLX) IPO." Nasdaq.com.
Retrieved June 2, 2012 (http://www.nasdaq.com
/markets/ipos/company/netflix-inc-75377-26907).

Netflix, Inc. "The Netflix Prize Rules." NetflixPrize.com. Retrieved June 19, 2012 (http://www.netflixprize .com//rules).

Netflix, Inc. "News Releases." Netflix Media Center. Retrieved July 7, 2012 (https://signup.netflix.com /MediaCenter/Press).

O'Brien, Jeffrey M. "The Netflix Effect." *Wired*, December 2002. Retrieved July 20, 2012 (http://www.wired.com /wired/archive/10.12/netflix.html?pg=1&topic=& topic_set=).

Rivlin, Gary. "Does the Kid Stay in the Picture?" *New York Times*, February 22, 2005. Retrieved July 20, 2012 (http://www.nytimes.com/2005/02/22/business /businessspecial/22rivl.html?_r=2&pagewanted =all&position=).

Summer, Nick. "Ted Sarandos' High-Stakes Gamble to Save Netflix." *Newsweek*, May 14, 2012. Retrieved July 20, 2012 (http://www.thedailybeast.com /newsweek/2012/05/13/ted-sarandos-high-stakes -gamble-to-save-netflix.html).

Tedeschi, Bob. "Blockbuster Dips Its Toe into DVD Subscriptions, Driving Down Netflix Stock. But the Threat May Lie Elsewhere." *New York Times*, August 12, 2002. Retrieved July 20, 2012 (http://www. nytimes.com/2002/08/12/business/e-commerce -report-blockbuster-dips-its-toe-into-dvd-subscriptions -driving-down.html?pagewanted=all&src=pm).

Thompson, Nicholas. "Netflix Uses Speed to Fend Off
Wal-Mart Challenge." *New York Times*, September 29,
2003. Retrieved July 20, 2012 (http://www
.nytimes.com/2003/09/29/business/media-netflix
-uses-speed-to-fend-off-wal-mart-challenge.html
?pagewanted=all&src=pm).

Index

ABOUT THE AUTHOR

Corinne Grinapol is a writer living in Brooklyn, New York. She studied international relations at the State University of New York at Geneseo. As a former research intern at the Woodrow Wilson International Center for Scholars, Grinapol has a deep appreciation for using primary documentation to help construct a narrative—as she did in this book by using Netflix's financial statements to look at the story the company told about itself.

PHOTO CREDITS

Cover, p. 3 Justin Sullivan/Getty Images; p. 7 © Martin E. Klimek/ZUMA Press; pp. 10–11, 15 iStockphoto/Thinkstock; p. 12 U.S. Marine Corps photo by Lance Cpl. John Kennicutt; p. 20 © Universal/courtesy Everett Collection; pp. 24–25, 29, 50–51, 70–71, 77, 84 © AP Images; pp. 26–27 AFP/Getty Images; pp. 34, 55, 82, 102 Bloomberg/Getty Images; pp. 36–37 Chris Hondros/Getty Images; p. 38 Karen Bleier/AFP/Getty Images; p. 43 Scott Olson/Getty Images; p. 52 Craig Mitchelldyer; pp. 58, 64–65 Jason Kempin/Getty Images; p. 66 © Brendan McDermid/ Reuters /Landov; p. 75 PRNewsFoto/Netflix, Inc./AP Images; p. 91 Netflix, Inc./AP Images; p. 94 PatrickMcMullan.com/AP Images; p. 97 L. Cohen/WireImage/Getty Images; p. 99 George Frey/Getty Images; pp. 104–105 Gareth Cattermole/Getty Images; background image pp. 17, 18, 30, 39, 40, 47, 48, 59, 60, 62, 73, 74, 79, 86, 87, 89, 90, 95, 96, 100, 101, kentoh/Shutterstock .com; cover and remaining interior background image dpaint/ Shutterstock.com.

Designer: Brian Garvey; Editor: Bethany Bryan;
Photo Researcher: Amy Feinberg